BOAT

For Pat (alias Kooky) from
the author; with special thanks
and appreciation for the
chef d'oeuvre of bonté p. 135.

Christmas 1969

With 95 black and white and 3 colour photographs

KAYE & WARD, LONDON

PETER HEATON

BOAT

First published by
Kaye & Ward Limited
194–200 Bishopsgate, London EC2
1969

© 1969 Kaye & Ward Ltd for all new material. Other material, copyright as listed in
the Acknowledgements

SBN 7182 0802 1

Printed in England by
Jarrold & Sons Ltd, Norwich

ACKNOWLEDGEMENTS

I wish to thank the following publishing firms and agencies for permission to quote extracts from the following works:

The Wind in the Willows. Associated Book Publishers, 11 Fetter Lane, London, E.C.4; Charles Scribners'
  Sons, 597 5th Avenue, New York, 10017.
Sailing in a Nutshell. Arthur Barker Ltd, 5 Winsley St, London, W.1.
Venturesome Voyages. The Bodley Head, 9 Bow St, London, W.C.2.
The Fight of the Firecrest. Christy and Moore, 52 Floral St, London, W.C.2.
The Riddle of the Sands. Sidgwick and Jackson, 1 Tavistock Chambers, Bloomsbury Way, London, W.C.1.
Deep Water and Shoal. Jonathan Cape, 30 Bedford Square, London, W.C.1; Miss Nanine Joseph,
  200 West 54th St, N.Y. 10019.
The Rich Man's guide to the Riviera. Cassell and Company, 35 Red Lion Square, London, W.C.1; The
  Sterling Lord Agency, 660 Madison Avenue, New York, 10021.
Around the World Single-handed. Meredith Press, 1716 Locust St, Des Moines, Iowa, 50303.
The Eye of the Wind. Hodder and Stoughton, St Paul's House, Warwick Lane, E.C.4; Houghton Mifflin
  Inc., 2 Park St, Boston, 02107.
A Ballad of John Silver. The Society of Authors, 84 Drayton Gardens, London, S.W.10; the Macmillan
  Company, 866 3rd Avenue, New York, 10022.
Barrack Room Ballads. A. P. Watt and Son, 26 Bedford Row, London, W.C.1; Doubleday and Company,
  277 Park Avenue, New York, 10017.

I wish also to thank Rear-Admiral Sir Rowland Jerram, K.B.E., D.S.O., D.L. for permission to quote from *The Falcon on the Baltic*; Mrs John Moore for the *Sonnet for dead comrades*, and Mr Colin W. Martyr for the *Southseaman* extract; Messrs A. and C. Black for permission to reproduce their drawings of yachts on page 61 (from my own book *The Sea gets Bluer*).

I further wish to thank the following photographers, firms and agencies, for permission to use those photographs marked in the Contents list: Miss Eileen Ramsay, 8 Copperhill Terrace, Hamble, Hants; the Union Castle Line; 'Infoplan' Ltd of London; the Trustees of the National Maritime Museum, Greenwich; the U.S. Embassy, London; Dell Quay (Sales) Ltd, Bridham, Chichester; and Brabourne (Marine) Ltd of 115 Gray's Inn Rd, London, W.C.1. I also wish to thank the Trustees of the Will of the late J.H.C. Evelyn for permission to reproduce the portrait of John Evelyn by Sir Godfrey Kneller.

A large measure of thanks is due to Miss G. D. F. Wharton for typing and most valuable assistance and advice; as it is also to my publishers, however hackneyed it may be to thank one's publisher nowadays!

PHOTOGRAPHIC ACKNOWLEDGEMENTS

(a) By Eileen Ramsay; (b) by permission of Union Castle Line; (c) by permission of 'Infoplan' Limited of London, S.W.1; (d) by permission of the National Maritime Museum, Greenwich; (e) by permission of Brabourne (Marine) Ltd of London; (f) by permission of the U.S. Embassy, London; (g) by permission of the National Maritime Museum, Greenwich (the Greenwich Hospital Collection); (h) by permission of Dell Quay (Sales) Ltd, Chichester. The remainder by the compiler.

CONTENTS

6

7

ABOUT 'BOAT' . . . Peter Heaton

Sea-memories are often recalled by small things: a cleat; the shape of a bow; a curious sea mark; the arch of a sail; a gaunt crane against the sky; sparkling water in an estuary; and so there are many such photographs in this book. Man has designed and built nothing more lovely than a yacht; so there are pictures of yachts of all kinds. People are stimulated by contrasts. Nowhere do you find such contrasts as in sailing. Bad weather foretells itself by lowering clouds. The seas grow dark and menacing. And then the storm passes and our souls are refreshed by blue skies and glorious sunshine; and refreshed the more by contrast. Contrast plays an important part in this book.

The letterpress, while in no significant order, seeks with the photographs, to create a pattern of moods and contrasts to evoke memories and to stimulate. I have deliberately avoided trying to fit pictures and prose into any pre-arranged pattern. But the reader has the freedom of the seas, for it is a book to 'dip into' as well as to enjoy the experience of reading it through. The subject-matter ranges wide as the sea itself, because the literature of the sea, past and present, classic to contemporary, gives so vast a choice. Moods vary from the adventurous to the romantic; the humorous to the poetic, and from the pompous to the preposterous.

Once people have tasted the salt spindrift from a yacht's bow-wave, they are hooked for life. To them this book needs little introduction. To those as yet 'unhooked' it may, I hope, open the door ajar to another way of life. The sea brings countless benefactions, but it also teaches us humility (often whether we want to be taught or not!). Sailing people (probably the most international of all people), are straightforward people. Which is why I have called this collection of photographs and writings, simply – Boat. But whether or not it provokes further inquiry into the world of water, it will I hope give you my reader an hour or so in the mysterious pleasure of the atmosphere of boats. Above all else, this book is for your delight.

INITIATION

Nothing could seem more ill-omened than the first incident related in the log for 1850, at the very commencement of my novitiate.

The day the 'Leo', 3 tons, left the builder's yard, she was so carelessly moored by the man who had charge of her, that she grounded during the night on the edge of a camp-shed at Charlton, between the Marine Society's ship and the shore. Being a deep boat, only half-decked, and heavily ballasted, the tide flowed into and filled her. Words will not describe the intense feeling of disappointment and mortification I experienced when I went down the next morning to try my new boat, and saw only a few feet of the mast above water.

With assistance kindly rendered from the Society's ship, she was got up at the following low water, and taken to Greenwich to be cleared of the mud and filth with which she was well plastered inside.

Since that time I have launched two new vessels, and took the precaution to have them christened in due form; my neglect of that ceremony in the case of the 'Leo' being, no doubt, the pretext for Father Thames taking it into his own hands.

The first sail was as far as Gravesend and back, with a waterman in charge, and this was the only apprenticeship I served. A confiding kinsman, whose judgement was almost equal to my own, accompanied me, and, his opinion coinciding with mine, that there was nothing to do which we could not easily do ourselves, I resolved to dispense with pilotage services from that day as a waste of money.

My first attempt, with only the boy on board and a chart for guide, though a very mild and unambitious little cruise from Charlton to Erith and back, was not concluded without a narrow escape. Passing between the collier brigs off Charlton at 10 p.m. to anchor for the night, I made allowance for the two I wished to pass ahead of, and then discovered a third vessel at anchor by itself, upon which we were helplessly driven by the tide. Our masthead fouling his bowsprit, the 'Leo' was beginning to fill, when the crew of the brig got the mast clear and she righted.

The second cruise was regularly planned and more pretentious. It was voted a jolly thing to drop down to Gravesend on the afternoon of the one day, and start early next morning for a sail round the Nore, my confiding kinsman to do duty as mate upon this grand occasion.

Great was our rejoicing when the anchor was let go at Gravesend, after having providentially passed safely inside the ships to the anchorage below the Custom House. After tea, which was made in a bachelor's kettle on deck, all hands turned in – the boy, the bachelor's kettle, and sundries occupied the forecastle, in which there was just room for all when properly packed. We, the quarter-deckers, of course occupied the cabin. Though the boat was only 3 tons, each had a properly constructed berth 6 feet by 2 feet, with bed and leeboard complete. Nothing could be more comfortable, if you could only remember that the deck beams were within 6 inches of your head. What with glorious anticipations for the morrow, bright ideas that would not keep, must be communicated immediately, and what with laughing and giggling, being too hot and too cold, and the novelty of the situation generally, there was not a wink of sleep got all night.

CLEOPATRA AND HER BARGE

From *Lives of the Noble Grecians: Life of Anthony* (circa 1593), Plutarch

But yet she carried nothing with her wherein she trusted more than in herself, and in the charms and enchantment of her passing beauty and grace. Therefore, when she was sent unto by divers letters, both from Antonius himself and also from his friends, she made so light of it and mocked so much, that she scorned to set forward otherwise than to take her barge in the river of Cydnus; the poop whereof was of gold, the sails of purple, and the oars of silver which kept stroke in rowing after the sound of the musicke of flutes, howboys, citherns, viols, and such other instruments as they played upon in the barge. And now for the person of herself; she was laid under a pavilion of cloth of gold tissue, attired and apparelled like the goddess Venus commonly drawn in picture; and hard by her, on either hand of her, pretty fair boys apparelled as painters do set forth god Cupid, with little fans in their hands, with the which they fanned a wind upon her. Her Ladies and Gentlemen also, the fairest of them were apparelled like the Nymphs Nereids (which are the mermaids of the waters) and like the Graces, some steering the helm, others tending the tackle and ropes of the barge out of which there came a wonderful passing sweet savour of perfumes that perfumed the wharf's side, pestered with innumerable multitudes of people. Some of them followed the barge all alongst the riverside: others also ran out of the city to see her coming in. So that in the end there ran such multitudes of people one after another to see her that Antonius was left post alone in the market-place in his Imperial seat, and there went a rumour in people's mouths, that the goddess Venus was come to play with the god Bacchus, for the general good of all Asia.

THE START OF THE GALE   From *Typhoon*, Joseph Conrad

'A gale is a gale, Mr Jukes,' resumed the Captain, 'and a full-powered steam-ship has got to face it. There's just so much dirty weather knocking about the world, and the proper thing is to go through it with none of what old Captain Wilson of the Melita calls "storm strategy". The other day ashore I heard him hold forth about it to a lot of shipmasters who came in and sat at a table next to mine. It seemed to me the greatest nonsense. He was telling them how he outmanœuvred, I think he said, a terrific gale, so that it never came nearer than fifty miles to him. A neat piece of head-work he called it. How he knew there was a terrific gale fifty miles off beats me altogether. It was like listening to a crazy man. I would have thought Captain Wilson was old enough to know better.'

Captain MacWhirr ceased for a moment, then said, 'It's your watch below, Mr Jukes?'

Jukes came to himself with a start. 'Yes, sir.'

'Leave orders to call me at the slightest change,' said the Captain. He reached up to put the book away, and tucked his legs upon the couch. 'Shut the door so that it don't fly open, will you? I can't stand a door banging. They've put a lot of rubbishy locks into this ship, I must say.'

Captain MacWhirr closed his eyes.

He did so to rest himself. He was tired, and he experienced that state of mental vacuity which comes at the end of an exhaustive discussion that had liberated some belief matured in the course of meditative years. He had indeed been making his confession of faith, had he only known it; and its effect was to make Jukes, on the other side of the door, stand scratching his head for a good while.

Captain MacWhirr opened his eyes.

He thought he must have been asleep. What was that loud noise? Wind? Why had he not been called? The lamp wriggled in its gimbals, the barometer swung in circles, the table altered its slant every moment; a pair of limp sea-boots with collapsed tops went sliding past the couch. He put out his hand instantly and captured one.

Jukes's face appeared in a crack of the door: only his face, very red, with staring eyes. The flame of the lamp leaped, a piece of paper flew up, a rush of air enveloped Captain MacWhirr. Beginning to draw on the boot, he directed an expectant gaze at Jukes's swollen, excited features.

'Came on like this,' shouted Jukes, 'five minutes ago . . . all of a sudden'.

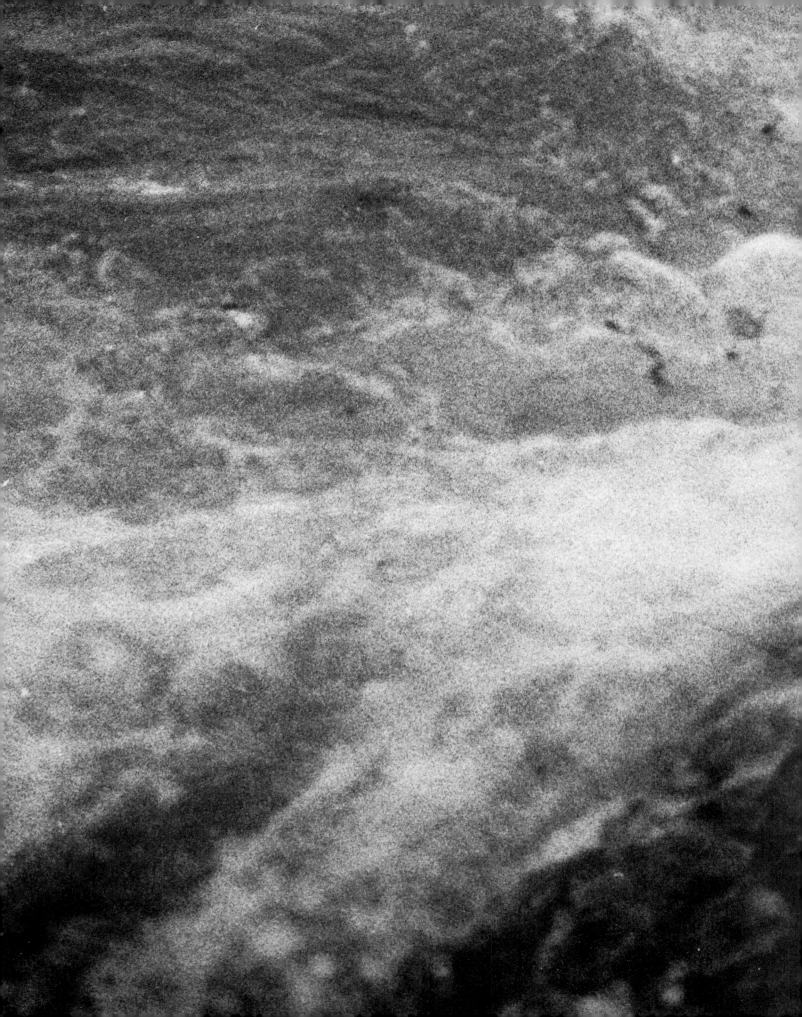

SONNET FOR DEAD COMRADES

John Moore

I am the tomb of one shipwrecked; but sail thou; for even while we perished, the other ships sailed on across the sea.

From *The Greek Anthology*

The world was young when this young sailor died
And the long ships were as new as a child's toy
To him who sailed at Odysseus' side,
Perhaps, from Ithaca to fabulous Troy.
O world too young, too fair, too bright for leaving
When the swift storm blew up, with the rocks a-lee
And the fanged white foam and the black waves heaving
Where grey-green olives meet the wine-dark sea!

But from his rosy-fingered dawn of day
Into our puzzled twilight, clear as a bell
His voice speaks plain the words which you would say
If to your shipmates you could bid farewell:
'Across the steep seas where I met my end
The ships sail on; and sail thou on, my friend.'

WINNING THE PRINCE OF WALES' CUP

From *The Eye of the Wind*, Peter Scott

John was covering Stewart so that in looking after one I was looking after them both. But my problem was suddenly complicated when John allowed Stewart to break tacks and go off on his own. My two most important rivals were now on opposite tacks. Which of them should I cover and make sure of keeping behind me? Stewart was four times winner of the Cup and was sailing 'Alarm', in which he had won the race in the two previous years. John had won the race once at Falmouth and was still sailing 'Lightning', the boat in which he had then triumphed. Since then he had twice been second in the same boat. 'Lightning' was older than 'Alarm' and if either was to get through it might be easier to catch 'Lightning' again. If I could not catch her it was John's turn to win rather than Stewart's and victory for so old a boat as 'Lightning' would be good for the class and maintain the value of second-hand boats. I decided to let John go, and tacked to cover Stewart. The wind was altering all the time very slightly; now that John was on the opposite tack to us any small alteration of wind which headed us on our tack freed him up on his and doubled the effect of the alteration on the relative positions of the two boats. This could work the other way, too, and might have favoured us, but as it turned out the next time we came together with John, he crossed ahead of us and was in the lead at the weather mark. There was little change on the next two reaches except that John opened out from us and rounded the leeward mark almost exactly one minute ahead. By now the tide had fallen slack and it was no longer necessary to go close inshore. We were going to have the whole sea for manœuvre on the last beat to the finishing line. As we came to the buoy with one more mile of windward work ahead of us, I said to my crew, 'It is a pity we couldn't win, but it's rather nice that old John in his four-year-old boat should be winning it don't you agree?' This released a tirade from Charles, the gist of which was that he had never expected to hear such defeatist talk from me, that it was absurd to say that the race was already won and why didn't we get on with it?

'But', said I, 'you know as well as I do that with competent operators in boats as nearly even as these are it is not possible to pick up a minute in a mile.'

'Well, you'll never know whether it is or not if you don't try!'

And so we set to and tried as never before; and at that critical moment there came a freshening of the breeze. After a couple of tacks we were sitting full out to keep the boat upright and driving her as hard as we could go. At the same time John and Tom Paxton (who were a good deal lighter than the combined weight of Charles Curry and me) were beginning to look back over their shoulders – beginning to realise that the freshening wind could beat them yet. Perhaps they were getting a little tired too, and earlier in the year John's appendix had been removed, which may have been a factor. Whatever the reasons, there came a time when the impossible seemed almost within our grasp. Up till now we had been carefully covering Stewart as well, and John of course had been covering us – tack for tack. Now we decided to wriggle and try to escape from John's control. We took a couple of short tacks, got him slightly out of step and unbelievably we were through. On the next port tack, we crossed his bows by about five yards, tacked to cover him, killed him with our wind shadow and crossed the finishing line sixteen seconds ahead of him after a race of three and a half hours. Twenty-two seconds after 'Lightning' came 'Alarm', closely followed by James Beale and Mrs Richardson.

It was a moment of immense elation. During the last minutes of the race there had been no time to savour the golden instant when we took the lead again. Now the gun had gone: the unbelievable had happened; at the fourth attempt we had won the Big Race. The years of failure had perhaps built it up to a disproportionate significance. But even now I look back on those few minutes after the finishing gun as among the most triumphant and utterly satisfying moments of my life.

Note: The race described was in 1937 at Lowestoft. 'Lightning', 'Alarm' and Peter Scott's boat 'Thunder' were, like all the other boats in this famous cup race, dinghies of the 14-foot International Class. 'Thunder', the winner, was designed and built by Uffa Fox.

MONTE CARLO

From *The Rich Man's guide to the Riviera*, David Dodge

From France, which surrounds Monaco on three sides and towers over it on one, you look down on a small rectangular harbour lying among three towns that run together at the edges like pancakes poorly poured: La Condamine at the base of the harbour, Monte Carlo on a bluff to its left, Monaco-Ville on a rock to the right. . .

It was François Blanc who founded the Société des Bains de Mer, built roads to improve communications between Monaco and nearby cities, promoted the attractions of Monte Carlo and brought to it the big spenders that were to make its fortune and his own. Around the roulette wheels of his day it was said, sometimes 'rouge' wins, sometimes 'noir' wins, always Blanc wins. He was a multimillionaire on other people's money when he died, leaving the business and its ill-will to his son Camille.

People were calling François Blanc names like minion of hell and purveyor of perdition before he even got fairly started in Monaco. In France, where roulette was illegal until 1934, pamphleteers attacked him variously as Satan, a genius of evil and the operator of a cathedral of vice. Others spoke of his early-day Disneyland as the moral cesspool of Europe. Billboards were rented around his borders to display pictures of the weeping widows of suicides he had caused and the removal of their orphaned children to cheerless institutions. An English visitor to Monaco charged him with maintaining '. . . a large house of sin blazing with gas lamps by night, flaming and shining by the shore, like pandemonium or the habitation of some romantic witch. The air swoons with the scent of lemon groves, tall palm trees wave their branches in the garden, music of the softest, most inebriating passion swells from the palace, rich meats and wines are served in a gorgeously furnished hall. . . Splendid women with bold eyes and golden hair and marble columns of imperial throats are there to laugh, to sing songs, to tempt . . .' – in short, wow-WEE! Monte Carlo couldn't have kept business away with a baseball bat if it had tried, and it wasn't trying. . .

The Summer Sporting Club is the stage for Monaco's annual gala ball in support of the Red Cross and other charities. If you have never been invited to one of these you have simply failed to make the social grade. They can be crashed, of course, but it isn't the same as appearing on the official form-sheet. The Prince and Princess are hosts at the Red Cross party, and the guest list usually encompasses tidy titles like those of the Maharani of Baroda, the Archduke Otto of Hapsburg, Prince Juan Carlos of Spain, the Maharaja of Indore, the Aga Khan, the Begum

of Palampur, the Nizam of Hyderabad and the Empress of Assam. Plain folk like the Môme Moineau, Mme Callas, Mr Onassis, and visiting celebrities of the stage and cinema world (including a Japanese girl who once signed the guest register as Miss Mitsi Pushover) also receive regular bids to the 'fête', and when approximately a thousand extroverted personalities with those Dun and Bradstreet ratings assemble in their party clothes on the moonlit terraces of a flower-bedecked gambling casino for champagne and charity, their combined glitter lights up the night sky like the Aurora Borealis. Mme Benitez-Rexach appeared at one benefit for the impoverished in a gown her 'couturière' had taken five months to create, for one wearing, from two hundred and fifty metres of nylon tulle and some thousands of small diamonds. Other guests at the annual alms-gathering may be a bit less twinkly than Kid Sparrow, but they are no less eager than she to contribute to the cause of charity. Big-name entertainments, jewelled door prizes, sustained firework displays and dancing until dawn mark the occasion, and when you have at last slipped away to your yacht in Monaco harbour and are adding up your good works for the evening before popping off to sleep between your silken sheets, warm in the knowledge that Ari and the Môme and the Maharani and Karim and Hapsie-Pooh and Nam and Juanito and the rest of your friends are moored all around you in *their* yachts drowsily thinking over *their* good works, it really makes you feel grateful that poor people were invented to do things for. The Riviera wouldn't be the same without them.

33

OCEAN

Childe Harold's Pilgrimage, Lord Byron

Thou glorious mirror, where the Almighty's form
Glasses itself in tempests; in all time,
Calm or convulsed – in breeze, or gale, or storm,
Icing the pole, or in the torrid clime
Dark-heaving; – boundless, endless, and sublime –
The image of Eternity – the throne
Of the Invisible; even from out thy slime
The monsters of the deep are made; each zone
Obeys thee; thou goest forth, dread, fathomless, alone.

And I have loved thee, Ocean! and my joy
Of youthful sports was on thy breast to be
Borne, like thy bubbles, onward: from a boy
I wanton'd with thy breakers – they to me
Were a delight; and if the freshening sea
Made them a terror – 'twas a pleasing fear,
For I was as it were a child of thee,
And trusted to thy billows far and near,
And laid my hand upon thy mane – as I do here.

AROUND THE WORLD SINGLE HANDED

From Harry Pidgeon's account of how he built his own boat 'Islander' and sailed Round the World in her . . .

The Islander was my first attempt at building a sail-boat, but I don't suppose there ever was an amateur-built craft that so nearly fulfilled the dream of her owner, or that a landsman ever came so near to weaving a magic carpet of the sea.

About this time I came across the plan of a boat that seemed to be very sea-worthy and, in addition, was not too large for one man to handle. Moreover, the construction of it did not seem too difficult for my limited knowledge of shipbuilding. Business with lumbermen and tourists in the big woods, and the proceeds from the sale of a small farm, put me in possession of the necessary funds, so I decided to build my long-dreamed-of ship and go on a voyage to the isles of the sea. From the mountains I went down to the shore of Los Angeles Harbour, located on a vacant lot, and began the actual work of construction.

'Why did you do it?' is the question that I am most often asked in regard to my sailing alone. One of the best reasons I had was the lack of means with which to buy a larger vessel and hire a crew to sail it for me. There is also a great satisfaction in accomplishing something by one's own effort. Men have often said to me, 'That is what I have always dreamed of doing, but you have done it.' During my long voyage I met several parties that were seeing the world from the decks of beautiful yachts, surrounded by friends and the luxuries that wealth will buy; but none of them seemed to be getting the thrill of joy out of it that I was in my little yawl.

It was shortly after midnight on the morning of January 10. It was a clear night, and the moon was full. The wind was blowing fresh, and there was a lump of a sea running. The Islander was cruising along under jib and mizzensail, and I was down below sound asleep, when we struck something with a crash. I sprang up to see the dark hull of a steamer looming alongside. My first thought was that she had run into my vessel, but she was going on the same course as the Islander, and at the same speed. If the crew had seen my boat in time to slow down, why had they not kept away? I threw the tiller over and tried to bring my boat up into the wind, but she was in too close contact. There I was with my boat on the windward side of the steamer, and every sea washing her up and down the iron side. In one of her upward rushes the foremast speared the steamer's bridge. In the bright moonlight I saw a row of faces lined up along the steamer's waist and peering down at me. Just then someone threw a large line, that hit me on the head, and an inquiring voice said, 'Have a rope.' For a moment I was dazed, and then it began to dawn on me that I was expected to leave my ship and its contents and climb up the rope! Actually they were trying to rescue me.

I was somewhat excited, so my answer was not very polite! 'What do I want with your rope?'

An officer on the bridge inquired, 'Don't you want assistance?'

'I want you to get out of this; go ahead, back up, or do something! ! ! !'

About that time a big wave came along, and I thought that I was going to board the steamer and take my ship along with me. For a moment the Islander was up on the steamer's rail, then the backwash from the side of the steamer threw her off, and she came up into the wind and ran clear. As she rounded to into the wind, the steamer came rolling back towards her, striking the end of the mizzen boom and breaking the gooseneck.

I was not alongside more than five minutes, but it was the most thrilling five minutes of my voyage.

UP ANCHOR

The cable being brought to, 'Heave round the capstan.' When the cable is perpendicular, the word is passed from forward, 'Up and down,' and immediately the anchor has broken out of the ground, 'Heave and aweigh.' The man at the lead in the chains reports as the ship is moving astern. See the helm amidships. As she gathers sternway her head will be forced to port by the sails on the foremast. Hoist the jibs immediately that they will take the proper way, and haul aft the sheets (it is sometimes necessary to haul aft the weather head sheets. Man the 'head braces and spanker outhaul'. As the after sails lift, 'Brace round the head yards.' Haul out the spanker. If the ship's head pays off too far, do not brace the head yards sharp up at once, and ease off the head sheets. As she comes to, brace up the head yards, and haul aft the head sheets. When the anchor is at the water's edge, the word is passed from forward, 'Heaving in sight,' and when up, 'Avast heaving.' 'Stand to the bars.' 'Stopper the cable.' 'Walk back the capstan.' Off nippers, or haul the cable off the capstan, bitt it, hook the cat. 'Man the cat-fall.' 'Haul taut the cat.' When the cat is taut, 'Keep hauling the cat.' Off slip stopper, 'Surge the cable,' and proceed as before described.

MAKE SAIL

'Overhaul the gear of the courses.' The leechlines and slablines are well overhauled by men on the lower yards; the bunt-lines having been stopped and hauled up in the top, ready to let run. Man the 'fore and main tacks,' 'Haul taut,' 'Ease down' the clewgarnets, 'Haul on board' the fore and main tacks, haul aft the sheets. 'Man the lee braces.' Brace the yards sharp up, haul taut the weather braces, lifts, and trusses. 'Haul the bowlines.'

PREPARATION FOR ACTION

Send top-gallant masts and yards on deck, as well as all running rigging that can be spared, studding sail booms, top gallant rigging, unbend or wet the sails, get down fore and mizen topsail yards, house the topmasts, lash them to the lower masts; pass a hawser round outside the rigging ready for frapping in a wreck, snake the stays and backstays, toggle the braces, yards braced sharp up, anchors lashed, boom boats ready for hoisting out, bowsprit and jibboom run in, spare wheel ropes rove, relieving tackles on, preventer stays on the masts, etc.

ON RUNNING AGROUND (SHOREGOING OR GROUNDWORK)

From *Sailing in a Nutshell*, Patrick Boyle

You will notice that the conversation of the complete and experienced yachts-man is freely interlarded with such expressions as 'grounded,' 'aground,' 'went ashore,' 'took the ground,' 'was cast up,' 'piled up,' 'wrecked,' 'flotsam and jetsam,' 'left high and dry,' 'buying another boat,' 'on the mud,' 'a thorough grounding in seamanship,' 'unlucky,' 'deceived by the chart,' and so on. From the frequency with which such terms occur you will realize that the process which they indicate is one with which no competent yachtsman is unfamiliar. Naturally, therefore, you will wish to know all about it, and this is accordingly designed to put the whole business in a nutshell (and/or cockleshell), starting at the surface and working downwards to the bottom (a procedure the reverse of normal, but common enough in nautical experience).

Briefly, running aground, or grounding, is the science of getting a boat stuck on the bottom without submerging, or even, if the helmsman has sufficient skill, out of the water altogether.

It is useful as a cure for seasickness or as a convenient means of exposing the bottom of the boat for the purpose of removing seaweed, barnacles and other unearned increment. As a matter of fact, the whole operation of going on the mud is extremely simple and can be performed merely by doing nothing in the right way and at the right time. If you hold the tiller quite still and till the vessel steadily ahead, no matter where you may happen to be at the moment, a satis-factory stranding – yet another word for the same thing – is bound almost in-variably to occur. You must not, however, then rest on your laurels, back, floor-boards or cabin seat and beam in a satisfied and complacent manner at your crew. Sea law (spelt lore) decrees that you immediately attempt to get afloat again, and it is now that the real fun begins; now that man begins to pit his wits against the merciless elements in the effort to wrest yet another victory from the sea.

There are few better ways of learning to do a thing than that of watching someone else – someone who understands the job – doing that thing well. Let us consider for a little, therefore, this boat coming down the river towards the sea. . . The helmsman is standing up, grim determination in every line of his face. . . The crew wear a slightly worried look. Or perhaps it is disappointment, for, contrary to their expectations, they are still afloat. However, they know their man and are confident that he will put them ashore at an early opportunity.

Yet notwithstanding their confidence, this time they form a tacit conspiracy to assist their captain, and as they sweep towards the shore in a welter of foam and spray all remain perfectly silent and inert. The only sound is provided by the roaring of the ship through the water and the screaming of the wind through the rigging. Suddenly, the bowsprit rises smartly into the air and remains there, the man standing on it falls into the water and the boat is at rest.

There follows a brief pause while the man at the helm, according to custom, ascertains that he has sustained no lasting injury and utters a series of well-rounded seamanlike oaths; and then ensues a scene of what appears to the uninitiated to be unparalleled confusion. Events move so swiftly that it is impossible for the untrained eye of the lay observer to follow them. One obtains an impression of one man swimming and of dozens dancing on the end of the bowsprit, dozens on the end of the boom, dozens pushing with boathooks and spars, dozens rowing away in the dinghy with an anchor on the end of a rope (or rope's end). And suddenly – all is still. It is recognised that the boat is well and truly aground and that, since they are both high and dry, a small glass of ale would not come amiss. There they are until the tide comes up again. Moreover, since it was a particularly high, or 'spring', tide, it will not come up so high again for a fortnight. A good job, in fact, well done.

THE 'CAPE OF STORMS'

From *Sailing alone around the world*, Captain Joshua Slocum

The Cape of Good Hope was now the most prominent point to pass. From Table Bay I could count on the aid of brisk trades, and then the 'Spray' would soon be at home. On the first day out from Durban it fell calm, and I sat thinking about these things and the end of the voyage. The distance to Table Bay, where I intended to call, was about eight hundred miles over what might prove a rough sea. The early Portuguese navigators, endowed with patience, were more than sixty-nine years struggling to round this cape before they got as far as Algoa Bay, and there the crew mutinied. They landed on a small island, now called Santa Cruz, where they devoutly set up the cross, and swore they would cut the captain's throat if he attempted to sail farther. Beyond this they thought was the edge of the world, which they too believed was flat; and, fearing that their ship would sail over the brink of it, they compelled Captain Diaz, their commander, to retrace his course, all being only too glad to get home. A year later, we are told, Vasco Da Gama sailed successfully round the 'Cape of Storms', as the Cape of Good Hope was then called, and discovered Natal on Christmas or Natal Day; hence the name. From this point the way to India was easy.

Gales of wind sweeping round the cape even now were frequent enough, one occurring, on an average, every thirty-six hours; but one gale was much the same as another, with no more serious result than to blow the 'Spray' along on her course when it was fair, or blow her back somewhat when it was ahead. On Christmas, 1897, I came to the pitch of the cape. On this day the 'Spray' was trying to stand on her head, and she gave me every reason to believe that she would accomplish the feat before night. She began very early in the morning to pitch and toss about in a most unusual manner, and I have to record that, while I was at the end of the bowsprit reefing the jib, she ducked me under water three times for a Christmas box. I got wet and did not like it a bit: never in any other sea was I put under more than once in the same short space of time, say three minutes. A large English steamer passing ran up the signal, 'Wishing you a Merry Christmas.' I think the captain was a humorist; his own ship was throwing her propeller out of water.

Two days later, the 'Spray', having recovered the distance lost in the gale, passed Cape Agulhas in company with the steamship Scotsman, now with a fair wind. The keeper of the light on Agulhas exchanged signals with the 'Spray' as she passed, and afterward wrote me at New York congratulations on the completion of the voyage. He seemed to think the incident of two ships of so

widely different types passing his cape together worthy of a place on canvas, and he went about having the picture made. So I gathered from his letter. At lonely stations like this hearts grow responsive and sympathetic, and even poetic. This feeling was shown toward the 'Spray' along many a rugged coast, and reading many a kind signal thrown out to her gave one a grateful feeling for all the world.

One more gale of wind came down upon the 'Spray' from the west after she passed Cape Agulhas, but that one she dodged by getting into Simons Bay. When it moderated she beat around the Cape of Good Hope, where they say the Flying Dutchman is still sailing. The voyage then seemed as good as finished; from this time on I knew that all, or nearly all, would be plain sailing.

Here I crossed the dividing-line of weather. To the north it was clear and settled, while south it was humid and squally, with, often enough, as I have said, a treacherous gale. From the recent hard weather the 'Spray' ran into a calm under Table Mountain, where she lay quietly till the generous sun rose over the land and drew a breeze from the sea.

The steam-tug 'Alert', then out looking for ships, came to the 'Spray' off Lion's Rump, and in lieu of a larger ship towed her into port. The sea being smooth, she came to anchor in the bay off the city of Cape Town, where she remained a day, simply to rest clear of the bustle of commerce. The good harbourmaster sent his steam-launch to bring the sloop to a berth in dock at once, but I preferred to remain for one day alone, in the quiet of a smooth sea, enjoying the retrospect of the passage of the two great capes. On the following morning the 'Spray' sailed into the Alfred Dry Docks, where she remained for about three months in the care of the port authorities, while I travelled the country from Simons Town to Pretoria, being accorded by the colonial government a free railroad pass over all the land.

The trip to Kimberley, Johannesburg, and Pretoria was a pleasant one. At the last-named place I met Mr Krüger, the Transvaal president. His excellency received me cordially enough; but my friend Judge Beyers, the gentleman who presented me, by mentioning that I was on a voyage around the world, unwittingly gave great offence to the venerable statesman, which we both regretted deeply. Mr Krüger corrected the judge rather sharply, reminding him that the world is flat. 'You don't mean *round* the world,' said the president; 'it is impossible! You mean *in* the world. Impossible!' he said, 'impossible!' and not another word did he utter either to the judge or to me. The judge looked at me and I looked at the judge, who should have known his ground, so to speak, and Mr. Krüger glowered at us both. My friend the judge seemed embarrassed, but I was delighted; the incident pleased me more than anything else that could have happened. It was a nugget of information quarried out of Oom Paul, some of whose sayings are famous. Of the English he said, 'They took first my coat and then my trousers.' He also said, 'Dynamite is the corner-stone of the South African Republic.' Only unthinking people call President Krüger dull.

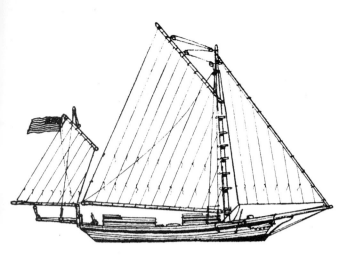

SPRAY

After her rig was altered in South American
waters; by shortening bowsprit and boom, and adding
mizzen-sail to form the Yawl rig shown here.
Length overall: 36 feet 9 inches
Beam: 14 feet 2 inches; 9 tons net
(A flying jib could be set on a bamboo lashed to the bowsprit)

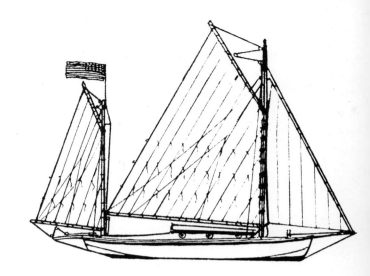

ISLANDER

Length overall: 34 feet
Beam: 10 feet 9 inches
Draught: 5 feet. Sail area: 630 square feet
This vessel, like the *Sea Queen* (see
Chapter 5) was of a type developed by
Captain Thomas Fleming Day and the
designing staff of *Rudder Magazine*.
They were designed for amateur
building, and Pidgeon built her himself.

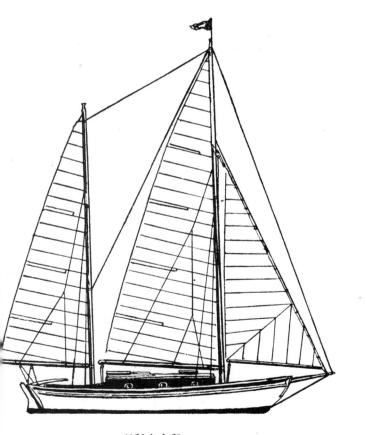

SVAAP

Length overall: 32 feet 6 inches
Length water-line: 27 feet 6 inches
Beam: 9 feet 6 inches. Draught: 5 feet 6 inches
Designed by John Alden, Boston

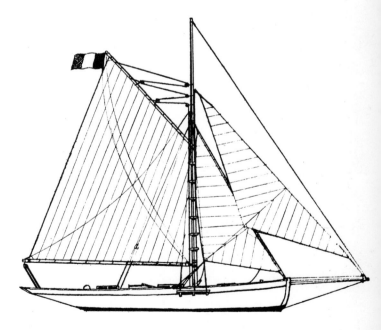

FIRECREST

Length overall: 39 feet
Length water-line: 30 feet
Beam: 8 feet 6 inches. Draught: 7 feet
Designed by Dixon Kemp
Built by P. T. Harris, at Rowhedge, Essex, in 1892
(After her Atlantic crossing she was converted to Bermudan rig)

WATER DEVILS   From *Anatomy of Melancholy*, Robert Burton 1576

Aerial spirits or devils, are such as keep quarter most part in the air, cause many tempests, thunders and lightenings . . . they cause whirlwinds on a sudden and tempestuous storms: which though our meteorologists generally refer to natural causes, yet I am of Bodine's mind, Thea. Nat. 1, 2, they are more often caused by those aerial devils in their several quarters: . . . These can corrupt the air, and cause plagues, sickness, storms, shipwrecks, fires, inundations . . . as for witches and sorcerers, in Lapland, Lithuania, and all over Scandinavia, to sell winds to mariners, and cause tempests which Marcus Paulus the Venetian relates likewise of the Tartars. . .

Water-devils are those naiads or water-nymphs which have been heretofore conversant about waters and rivers. The water (as Paracelsus thinks) is their chaos, wherein they live; some call them fairies, and say that Habundia is their Queen; these cause inundations, many times shipwrecks, and deceive men divers ways, as Succuba, or otherwise, appearing most part (saith Tritemius) in women's shapes. Paracelsus hath several stories of them that lived and been married to mortal men, and so continued for certain years with them, and after, upon some dislike, have forsaken them. Such a one was Egeria, with whom old Numa was so familiar, Diana, Ceres, etcetera. Olaus Magnus hath a long narration of one Hotherus, a king of Sweden, that having lost his company, as he was hunting one day, met with these Water-Nymphs or Fairies and was feasted by them: and Hector Boethius, of Macbeth and Banquo, two Scottish lords, that, as they were wandering in the woods, had their fortunes told them by three strange women. To these, heretofore, they did sacrifice by that ὑδρομαντεία or divination by waters.

Terrestrial devils are these Lares, Genii, Fauns, Satyrs, Wood-Nymphs, Foliots, Fairies, Robin Goodfellows, Trulli, etcetera, which as they are most conversant with men, so they do them most harm. . .

Nero and Heliogabalus, Maxentius, and Julianus Apostata, were never so much addicted to magic of old, as some of our modern princes and Popes themselves are nowadays. Erricus King of Sweden had an enchanted cap, by virtue of which, and some magical murmur or whispering terms he could command spirits, trouble the air, and make the wind sound which way he would, insomuch that when there was any great wind or storm, the common people were wont to say, the King now had on his conjouring cap. But such examples are infinite, that which they can do, is as much almost as the devil himself, who is still ready to satisfy the desires, to oblige them the more unto him. They can cause tempests, storms, which is familiarly practised by witches in Norway, Iceland, as I have proved. . .

CAN'T YOU DANCE THE POLKA?

SOLOIST:

As I walked down the Broadway, One ev'ning in Ju-ly I met a maid, she asked my trade, "A sail-or lad" quoth I___

CHORUS:

And a-way, yo' san-tee, my dear An-nie. Oho! You New York gals, Can't you dance the pol-ka?

2. To Nelligan's I took her,
   I did not spare expense;
   I bought her a slap-up supper
   That cost me ninety cents.
     Chorus: And away yo' santee, etc.

3. Said she. 'You lime-juice sailor,
   Now see me home you may.'
   But when at last we reached her door,
   Then to me she did say.
     Chorus: And away, yo' santee, etc.

4. 'My flash man he's a Yankee,
   With his hair clipped down behind;
   He wears a brass-bound jacket,
   And sails in the Blackball Line.'
     Chorus: And away, yo' santee, etc.

5. 'He's homeward bound this evening,
   And with me he will stay,
   So kiss me, dear, for much I fear,
   You'll have to sail away.'
     Chorus: And away, yo' santee, etc.

6. I kissed her hard and proper
   Before her flash man came,
   And said, 'Farewell, you naughty gel,
   I know your little game.'
     Chorus: And away, yo' santee, etc.

70

TOM'S GONE TO HILO

SOLOIST ... CHORUS
Tom-my's gone and I'll go too A-
way down Hi-lo____ SOLOIST Oh, Tom-my's
CHORUS gone, and I'll go too Tom's gone to Hi-lo.____

2. Tommy's gone to Mobile Bay
  Chorus: Away, etc.
  Oh, Tommy's gone to Mobile Bay
  Chorus: Tom's gone, etc.

3. Tommy's gone to Trafalgar.
  Oh Tommy's gone to Trafalgar.

4. The Old Victory led the way.
  The Brave Old Victory led the way.

5. Tommy's gone for evermore,
  Oh Tommy's gone for evermore.

6. He didn't kiss his lass goodbye,
  It broke her heart and made her cry.

It was on the third day out, and we were sailing near Wessel Island on the west side of the gulf, that I felt a sudden attack of painful cramp in my stomach. There was a fair medicine chest on board, and I resorted to various kinds of medicine which I deemed appropriate. But all salts, castor oil and similar strong remedies failed to bring relief. We had plenty of tinned fish on board, of which I had frequently eaten. Some of it must have been bad and thus became the source of my indisposition. I suffered terrible pain, and as I was unable to secure relief we steered in for Wessel Island, which we reached in a few hours. Luckily, we struck a good landing-place, with smooth water and a fine sandy beach clothed with bushy trees and green grass patches. We secured the 'Tilikum', and with the assistance of Mac I managed to get ashore. Under a shady tree I dropped down on the grass. Added to the painful cramp, I now developed a very bad headache, and as by that time I was so weak that I felt sure my end was near at hand, I asked Mac to bring writing materials from the boat, as I wished to leave a testimonial to exonerate my mate from any blame in case I should die. Mac was squatting at my side, and on looking at him I could see that he felt nearly as bad as I did myself.

'I think I know of a remedy that will do you good,' he said.

'Then let me have it by all means, whatever it may be,' I replied hopefully.

'It will either cure or kill you,' Mac added.

'Then you had better get me the writing materials first,' I retorted, somewhat abashed.

'I will not,' he replied, 'but will run the risk and administer the medicine first!' and with that he went off to the boat.

Meantime I lay there, rolling about in convulsions, and thinking of the past, the present and the future. The awful pain racked my body, and I yelled for Mac to hurry with his medicine, for it seemed to me an hour since he had gone. On his return he said that it had taken him ten minutes to provide his 'kill or cure' remedy, which consisted of a cupful of hot water and a tablespoonful of Colman's mustard. These he mixed and ordered me to swallow immediately, and every drop of it!

Now, a little mustard with meat is all very well, and a little too much of it – we all know what that means. But when Mac told me to swallow his concoction I thought it would be impossible. Nevertheless, under the circumstances, and with Mac insisting that it must be taken at all costs, I raised the cup to my lips and drank the nauseous mixture! When half of it was down it endeavoured to return immediately. However, I was determined it should not, and in this matter

I was victorious. But the feelings that stormed within me it is impossible to describe. Mac was kneeling by my side and had reverted to his former calling, as I faintly noticed. My inside felt afire, and it seemed as if an explosion would take place in my stomach. I was just about to accuse Mac of killing me when suddenly I became very busy. I could hear Father Mac praying that I might be helped out of my misery, then 'Colman' got to work and before two minutes had elapsed nothing could possibly have been left in my stomach! I felt a wonderful relief, and after a short rest was myself again.

A ship is floating in the harbour now,
A wind is hovering o'er the mountain's brow;
There is a path on the sea's azure floor,
No keel has ever ploughed that path before;

The halcyons brood around the foamless isles;
The treacherous ocean has forsworn its wiles;
The merry mariners are bold and free:
Say, my heart's sister; will thou sail with me?

From Epipsychidion *by P. B. Shelley*

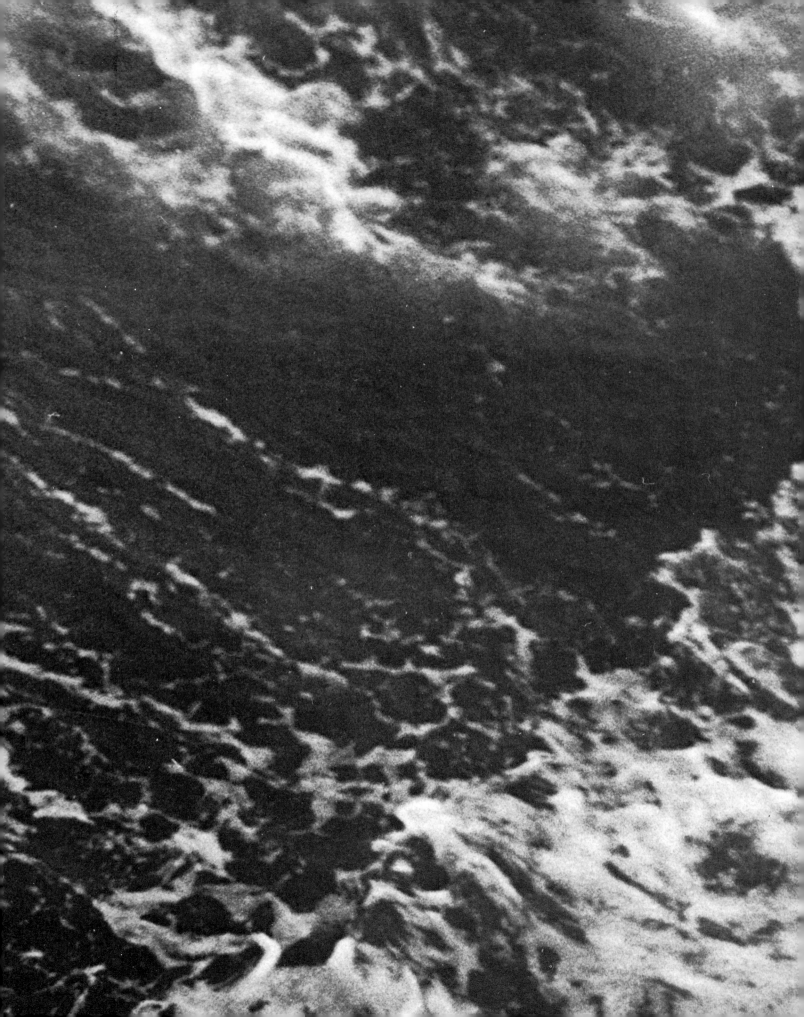

OCEAN

OCEAN
Childe Harold's Pilgrimage, Lord Byron

Roll on, thou deep and dark blue Ocean – roll!
Ten thousand fleets sweep over thee in vain;
Man marks the earth with ruin – his control
Stops with the shore; – upon the watery plain
The wrecks are all they deed, nor doth remain
A shadow of man's ravage, save his own,
When, for a moment, like a drop of rain,
He sinks into thy depths with bubbling groan,
Without a grave, unknell'd, uncoffin'd, and unknown.

OATS

2130

SLAUGHDEN
QUAY

HIGH WATER
AT THIS QUAY
TO DAY

AM

PM

JUMBO.

We now had practically clear sailing ahead of us to Tahiti, and only 390 miles to go. Luck had been with us in getting by the Dangerous Archipelago, for we had romped through in thirty hours instead of being delayed by the calms I had expected.

The next land we saw was the steep little island of Mehetia, sixty miles east of Tahiti, and when dawn came on January 6th, the great bulk of our goal loomed fifty miles distant, shrouded in haze and clouds. All day we gazed upon the astonishing mountains and gorges that grew ever larger and more spectacular ahead of us, while our breeze gradually deserted us and our hearts sank at the thought of another night at sea, and so close to port.

And then just at sunset our guardian angel sent a land breeze out to us laden with perfume. We approached the land and got within its protecting influence. We had the almost forgotten sensation of sailing in smooth waters. There are no smooth waters at sea.

Point Venus light, where Captain Cook made his famous observations, shone out for us, and all along the great barrier reef lights twinkled to guide us along the shore. We pondered at these reddish twinkling lights, and later found that they were the natives torch-fishing along the reef.

We ghosted along within sound of the surf, looking for Papeete, and suddenly there it was—a crescent of tiny lights. Becalmed directly off the town we unshipped the squaresail yard, unbent the sail and stowed it below. For a month this sail had been off but once, and then only thirty hours. It was worn. The yard lacing was temporarily patched in many places. The sail itself was practically blown out of the bolt-ropes half the way round. It would have to be almost remade before it could be used again. But if anyone should ask me I should say it was *some* sail.

Tahiti is entirely surrounded by a barrier reef which lies anywhere from a few yards to a half-mile or so from shore, upon which the sea almost always breaks heavily. There are passes here and there through which vessels may enter, but strong currents make caution necessary.

The Pilot Book says of the Papeete pass that one must take a pilot and enter by day. But there are two red range lights on shore that make it possible to come in at night, and I had a good chart of the harbour. We had been at sea just a month and had sailed 3,700 miles. The twinkling lights were a magnet that was irresistible.

So just after midnight we found the pass through the reef, brought the red lights to bear in a straight line, and ran in with the thunder of the surf on both sides. Once in the fairway along the shore we turned sharp east and slowly glided along the famous Papeete water-front, to tie up to a buoy in the inner harbour just off the government dock.

The air was heavy with the scent of lovely flowers, and there were strange land noises. We could hear a milkman making his way about town, and soon all the sounds of a community awakening. Birds, dogs, cattle – it was all so strange to us. I put up the quarantine flag and gave myself over to the ecstasy of it all – the glorious feeling that comes only at the end of such a voyage – a feeling of utter relaxation and peace, and of accomplishment.

One might almost say that Tahiti is inhabited by men who came for a vacation and stayed for ever. That is, of course, speaking of the white population. As for myself, I stayed eight months and was filled with regret when I finally watched the towering bulk of Tahiti and its sister island Moorea fade into the dusk of evening as we sailed out to sea again.

Hence in a season of calm weather
Though inland far we be
Our souls have sight of that immortal sea
Which brought us hither
Can in a moment travel thither
And see the children sport upon the shore
And hear the mighty waters rolling evermore.

From : Intimations of Immortality *by William Wordsworth*

THE EYE OF THE WIND

C. Day Lewis

Eye of the wind, whose bearing in
A changeful sky the sage
Birds are never wrong about
And mariners must gauge –

The drift of flight, the fluttered jib
Are what we knew it by:
Seafarers cannot hold or sight
The wind's elusive eye.

That eye, whose shifting moods inspire
The sail and trim the sheet,
Commands me, though I can but steer
Obliquely towards it.

IT'S ALL TOSH! (or you can't win)   Bill Whetton

'Well – I mean – all this about sailing being for the ordinary man is a lot of tosh!'

'If you spent less on birds and booze you could easy afford a dinghy.'

'I don't like the sound of that mate!'

'There's all sorts of things you can move on to once you've started, like.'

'Oh yeah! Such as?'

'Smuggling for instance. Nipping across the channel on a dark night, laden down with whisky to sell to the continentals at five quid a bottle!'

'If I did that it'd be something a bit more pricey than booze!'

'Then there's girls. Girls like sailors, they go for those big muscles in the arms and legs an' that faraway look at the blue horizon.'

'You know your trouble mate? You're a b—— romantic! "Blue horizon!" When did you see a blue horizon in England?'

'Last July at Southend.'

'Nine months ago! Blue skies! Anyway birds much prefer the back of a really fast bike – what kind of a ride can you get in a dinghy?'

'OK! then, but what about the gear on shore after the sail? All that groovy plastic in all those new nautical colours – boy!'

'Are you *trying* to be funny?'

'How about the millionaires you meet in the yacht clubs? A party for four, you and the millionaire and two birds under the Mediterranean awning swilling champagne?'

'You got any idea what them clubs cost?'

'Yeah! Quid a year some of 'em.'

'You won't meet many millionaires in that sort of joint!'

'Maybe not – but one thing leads to another –'

'I can just see it! "Good evening tosher what's your boat?" and he says "Oh I've got three actuallam! One in Florida; one in the Med and a small one of fifty tons at Cowes to slum in. What's yours?" and you say that you hire a dinghy once a month! Be your age!'

'You could maybe provide him with birds to sail with.'

'You've got a point boy! Big commission and a share of the profits!'

'You know the trouble about you? – You just don't like the new fashionable sport of yachtin!'

'Yes I do! I just don't like dinghies, I've got a forty-foot high speed motor-cruiser as it happens – at least my bird has.'

'Well then – for God's sake, what's all this conversation been about? I thought you said that all that about sailing being for the ordinary man was all tosh?'

'I did! An' it is! But I ain't no ordinary man, mate!'

SEA SERPENTS   From *A daring Voyage*, the Andrews Brothers

Wednesday, July 17th 1878 – Wind S.S.W.; course E. by S. half S.; sea smooth. These good weather spells kind of knock spots out of our ideas of making a quick passage. Just thirty-four days out. I never took much stock about sea serpents, but I have good reason to believe, after what I saw last evening, before dark, that there are denizens of the deep that have never been thoroughly explained or illustrated by our zoological societies. It was during a moment of intense calm, and I had been watching some whales sporting and spouting at a short distance behind me, when, on turning and looking in the opposite direction, I was startled to see what appeared to be a part of a huge monster in the shape of a snake; it was about two hundred feet off. I saw twelve or fifteen feet of what appeared to be the tail of a huge black snake from five to fifteen inches in diameter, the end being stubby, or round, and white. It was in the air in a corrugated shape in motion, and in the act of descending. I also saw a dark shadowy form in the water corresponding with the tail; also the wake on the water as if more had just gone down, the whole being in motion after the manner of a snake; also heard the noise of the descending part, and saw the splash on the water.

Walter being just at that moment at the cuddy, where I keep the hatchet, getting some tea for supper, I told him to pass me the hatchet quick, which he did. He heard the splash and saw the form in the water. I wanted the hatchet, not because I thought I should have to use it, but because I thought it would be a good thing to have it handy, in case I should want to use it. Walter had a swim an hour before near the boat, and the thought of sea serpents being around kind of took away his relish for that kind of sport for the present.

During the night we heard from time to time the most horrid noises behind us that we have ever heard on the water – splashing and breathing in a loud wheezy manner, but that we took to be whales. This morning we saw and heard whales beating the water with their tails three miles off, throwing the water to a great distance in the air. We thought if they only saw fit to give the 'Nautilus' one of those blows, that would settle our case here and save funeral expenses.

Thursday, July 18th – Wind light, E. and S.E. At daylight saw three sails on horizon bound to westward. We spoke the middle one, the British brigantine 'Nellie Crosby,' of Yarmouth, N.S., Captain Bain, from England to Baltimore, Md., long 24.30 W. Invited us on board to breakfast. Had a very sociable time; furnished us with a few luxuries we were in need of. No observation; rather chilly; we make but little easting. Last night Walter was taken with haemorrhage, coughing up considerable quantities of blood; he said he felt better after it apparently; continued bleeding through the night at intervals. We made about thirty miles. Captain Bain said he had seen several sea serpents.

Friday, July 19th – Light easterly winds, and we make considerable leeway; course doubtful. Passed between a brig and a brigantine about 8 a.m. bound west. Did not feel like speaking either of them, as we are in want of nothing but land. Fortune seems to have been against us from the send off, and we have given up all hopes of a quick passage. For twenty-six days the 'Nautilus' did not rest a moment that she could sail; but our ignorance of certain localities, and having to heave to so often, everything being saturated with water, discouraged us. A quick passage is possible now, but not probable. Our health has been good beyond expectation, outside of Walter's haemorrhage (I hardly understand *that* – he says he feels better every time after bleeding), neither of us being unable to perform our respective duties.

Although with a little reluctance for a moment sometimes, did we turn out of our 'cubby hole' into the cold wet storm and dense darkness with fog, for eighteen consecutive days and nights that we passed without sun, moon, or stars to cheer us, to perform our task of four hours or more at the helm, to keep a faithful look-out before and behind, and to watch the compass with the utmost scrutiny without having been fairly asleep; and if sleep did come it was disturbed by dreams of a restless imagination that we were even then on duty, and had been for a week, and about to be relieved, instead of being off duty and about to go on.

THE TEST
From *The Fight of the Firecrest*, Alain Gerbault

It was a dirty-looking morning on the 20th, and the climax of all the gales that had gone before. It was the day, too, when the 'Firecrest' came near to making the port of missing ships. As far as the eye could see there was nothing but an angry welter of water, overhung with a low-lying canopy of leaden, scurrying clouds, driving before the gale.

By ten o'clock the wind had increased to hurricane force. The seas ran short and viciously. Their curling crests racing before the thrust of the wind seemed to be torn into little whirlpools before they broke into a lather of soapy foam. These great seas bore down on the little cutter as though they were finally bent on her destruction. But she rose to them and fought her way through them in a way that made me want to sing a poem in her praise.

Then, in a moment, I seemed engulfed in disaster. The incident occurred just after noon. The 'Firecrest' was sailing full and by, under a bit of her mainsail, and jib. Suddenly I saw, towering on my limited horizon, a huge wave rearing its curling, snowy crest so high that it dwarfed all others I had ever seen. I could hardly believe my eyes. It was a thing of beauty as well as of awe as it came roaring down upon us.

Knowing that if I stayed on deck I would meet death by being washed overboard, I had just time to climb into the rigging, and was about half-way to the masthead when it burst upon the 'Firecrest' in fury, burying her from my sight under tons of solid water and a lather of foam. The gallant little boat staggered and reeled under the blow, until I began to wonder anxiously whether she was going to founder or fight her way back to the surface.

Slowly she came out of the smother of it, and the great wave roared away to leeward. I slid down from my perch in the rigging to discover that it had broken off the outboard part of the bowsprit. Held by the jibstay, it lay in a maze of rigging and sail under the less rail, where every sea used it as a battering ram against the planking, threatening, at every blow, to stave a hole in the hull.

The mast was also swaying dangerously as the 'Firecrest' rolled. Somehow the shrouds had become loose at the masthead. There was now a fair prospect that the cutter would roll the mast out of her, even if the broken bowsprit failed to stave the hole it seemed trying for. The wind cut my face with stinging force, and the deck was, most of the time, awash with breaking seas.

But I was obliged to jump to work to save both boat and life. First I had to get the mainsail off her, and, in trying to do so, found the hurricane held the sail so hard against the lee topping lift that I had to rig a purchase to haul it down with the downhaul; but I finally managed to get it stowed.

It proved a tremendous job to haul the wreckage aboard. The deck was like a slide, and the gale so violent that I had to crouch down in order to keep from being wrenched off the deck and hurled bodily into the sea. I clung desperately to the shrouds at intervals. The broken part of the bowsprit was terrifically heavy, and I had to lash a rope round it while it was tossing about and buffeting the side. Several times it nearly jerked me overboard.

At last I had the jib in, and the bowsprit safely lashed on deck; but it was nearly dusk and I felt worn out. . . It was now nearly dark and the gale seemed to be moderating a little, so I went below to get supper.

But when I tried to start a fire, neither of the two Primus stoves would work: so I had to turn in, hungry, cold, drenched and exhausted, for the first time on the cruise sad, fagged out and fed up.

GOLDEN DAYS AND BALMY NIGHTS!

From *The Wind in the Willows*, Kenneth Grahame

'My last voyage,' began the Sea Rat, 'that landed me eventually in this country, bound with high hopes for my inland farm, will serve as a good example of any of them, and, indeed, as an epitome of my highly-coloured life. Family troubles, as usual, began it. The domestic storm-cone was hoisted, and I shipped myself on board a small trading vessel bound from Constantinople, by classic seas whose every wave throbs with a deathless memory, to the Grecian Islands and the Levant. Those were golden days and balmy nights! In and out of harbour all the time – old friends everywhere – sleeping in some cool temple or ruined cistern during the heat of the day – feasting and song after sundown, under great stars set in a velvet sky! Thence we turned and coasted up the Adriatic, its shores swimming in an atmosphere of amber, rose and aquamarine; we lay in wide land-locked harbours, we roamed through ancient and noble cities, until at last one morning, as the sun rose royally behind us, we rode into Venice down a path of gold. O, Venice is a fine city, wherein a rat can wander at his ease and take his pleasure! Or, when weary of wandering, can sit at the edge of the Grand Canal at night, feasting with his friends, when the air is full of music and the sky full of stars, and the lights flash and shimmer on the polished steel prows of the swaying gondolas, packed so that you could walk across the canal on them from side to side! And then the food – do you like shell-fish? Well, well, we won't linger over that now . . .'

'Southward we sailed again at last, coasting down the Italian shore. . . . From Corsica, I made use of a ship that was taking wine to the mainland. We made Alassio in the evening, lay to, hauled up our wine-casks, and hove them overboard, tied one to the other by a long line. Then the crew took to the boats and rowed shorewards, singing as they went, and drawing after them the long bobbing procession of casks, like a mile of porpoises. On the sands they had horses waiting, which dragged the casks up the steep street of the little town with a fine rush and clatter and scramble. When the last cask was in, we went and refreshed and rested, and sat late into the night, drinking with our friends.'

DAVIES RUNS AGROUND IN A GALE

From *The Riddle of the Sands*, Erskine Childers

'We had been about level till then, but with my shortened canvas I fell behind. Not that that mattered in the least. I knew my course, had read up my tides, and, thick as the weather was, I had no doubt of being able to pick up the lightship. No change of plan was possible now. The Weser estuary was on my starboard hand, but the whole place was a lee-shore and a mass of unknown banks – just look at them. I ran on, the "Dulcibella" doing her level best, but we had some narrow shaves of being pooped. I was about *here*, say six miles south-west of the lightship, when I suddenly saw that the "Medusa" had hove to right ahead, as though waiting till I came up. She wore round again on the course as I drew level, and we were alongside for a bit. Dollmann lashed the wheel, leaned over her quarter, and shouted, very slowly and distinctly so that I could understand: "Follow me – sea too bad for you outside – short cut through sands – save six miles."

'It was taking me all my time to manage the tiller, but I knew what he meant at once, for I had been over the chart carefully the night before. You see the whole bay between Wangeroog and the Elbe is encumbered with sand. A great jagged chunk of it runs out from Cuxhaven in a north-westerly direction for fifteen miles or so, ending in a pointed spit called the Scharhorn. To reach the Elbe from the west you have to go right outside this, round the lightship, which is off the Scharhorn, and double back. Of course, that's what big vessels do. But, as you see, these sands are intersected here and there by channels, very shallow and winding, exactly like those behind the Frisian Islands. Now look at this one, which cuts right through the big chunk of sand and comes out near Cuxhaven. The Telte it's called. It's miles wide, you see, at the entrance, but later on it is split into two by the Hohenhörn bank; then its gets shallow and very complicated, and ends as a mere tidal driblet with another name. It's just the sort of channel I should like to worry into on a fine day or with an off-shore wind. Alone, in thick weather and a heavy sea, it would have been folly to attempt it, except as a desperate resource. But, as I said, I knew at once that Dollmann was proposing to run for it and guide me in.

'I didn't like the idea, because I like doing things for myself, and, silly as it sounds, I believe I resented being told the sea was too bad for me, which it certainly was. Yet the short cut did save several miles and a devil of a tumble off the Scharhorn, where two tides meet. I had complete faith in Dollmann, and I suppose I decided that I should be a fool not to take a good chance. I hesitated,

Peter Heaton

I know; but in the end I nodded and held up my arm as she forged ahead again. Soon after she shifted her course and I followed. You asked me once if I ever took a pilot. That was the only time.'

He spoke with bitter gravity, flung himself back and felt his pocket for his pipe. It was not meant for a dramatic pause, but it certainly was one. I had just a glimpse of still another Davies – a Davies five years older, throbbing with deep emotions, scorn, passion and stubborn purpose; a being above my plane, of sterner stuff, wider scope. Intense as my interest had become, I waited almost timidly while he mechanically rammed tobacco into his pipe and struck ineffectual matches. I felt that whatever the riddle to be solved, it was no mean one. He repressed himself with an effort, half rose and made his circular glance at the clock, barometer and skylight, and then resumed.

'We soon came to what I knew must be the beginning of the Telte channel. All round you could hear the breakers on the sands, though it was too thick to see them yet. As the water shoaled, the sea of course got shorter and steeper. There was more wind – a whole gale I should say.

'I kept dead in the wake of the "Medusa", but to my disgust I found she was gaining on me very fast. Of course I had taken for granted, when he said he would lead me in, that he would slow down and keep close to me. He could easily have done so by getting his men up to check his sheets or drop his peak. Instead of that he was busting on for all he was worth. Once, in a rain-squall, I lost sight of him altogether; got him faintly again, but had enough to do with my own tiller not to want to be peering through the scud after a runaway pilot. I was all right so far, but we were fast approaching the worst part of the whole passage, where the Hohenhörn bank blocks the road and the channel divides. I don't know what it looks like to you on the chart – perhaps fairly simple, because you can follow the twists of the channels, as on a ground-plan; but a stranger coming to a place like that (where there are no buoys, mind you) can tell nothing certain by the eye, unless perhaps at dead low water, when the banks are high and dry, and in very clear weather; he must trust to the lead and the compass and feel his way step by step. I knew perfectly well that what I should soon see would be a wall of surf stretching right across and on both sides. To *feel* one's way in that sort of weather is impossible. You must *know* your way, or else have a pilot. I had one, but he was playing his own game.

'With a second hand on board to steer while I conned I should have felt less of an ass. As it was, I knew I ought to be facing the music in the offing, and cursed myself for having broken my rule and gone blundering into this confounded short cut. It was giving myself away, doing just the very thing that you can't do in single-handed sailing.

'By the time I realized the danger it was far too late to turn and hammer out to the open. I was deep in the bottle-neck bight of the sands, jammed on a lee-shore, and a strong flood tide sweeping me on. That tide, by the way, gave just the ghost of a chance. I had the hours in my head, and knew it was about two-thirds flood with two hours more of rising water. That meant the banks would all be covering when I reached them, and harder than ever to locate; but it also meant that I *might* float right over the worst of them if I hit off a lucky place.' Davies thumped the table in disgust. 'Pah! It makes me sick to think of having to trust to an accident like that, like a lubberly Cockney out for a boosy Bank Holiday sail.

'Well, just as I foresaw, the wall of surf appeared clean across the horizon, and curling back to shut me in, booming like thunder. When I last saw the "Medusa" she seemed to be charging it like a horse at a fence, and I took a rough bearing of her position by a hurried glance at the compass. At that very moment I thought she seemed to luff and show some of her broadside; but a squall blotted her out and gave me hell with the tiller. After that she was lost in the white mist that hung over the line of breakers. I kept on my bearing as well as I could, but I was already out of the channel. I knew that by the look of the water, and as we neared the bank I saw it was all awash and without the vestige of an opening. I wasn't going to chuck her on to it without an effort; so, more by instinct than with any particular hope, I put the helm down, meaning to work her along the edge on the chance of spotting a way over. She was buried at once by the beam sea, and the jib flew to blazes; but the reefed stays'l stood, she recovered gamely, and I held on, though I knew it could only be for a few minutes as the centre-plate was up and she made frightful leeway towards the bank.

'I was half blinded by scud, but suddenly I noticed what looked like a gap, behind a spit which curled out right ahead. I luffed still more to clear this spit, but she couldn't weather it. Before you could say knife she was driving across it, bumped heavily, bucked forward again, bumped again, and – ripped on in deeper water! I can't describe the next few minutes. I was in some sort of channel, but a very narrow one, and the sea broke everywhere. I hadn't proper command either; for the rudder had crocked up somehow at the last bump. I was like a drunken man running for his life down a dark alley, barking himself at every corner. It couldn't last long, and finally we went crash on to something and stopped there, grinding and banging. So ended that little trip under a pilot.'

COTE d'AZUR From *The Rich Man's guide to the Riviera*, David Dodge

The Côte d'Azur has undergone some pretty radical changes during its career while remaining at all times très, très, cosmopolite. In Victoria's day a menial was a menial and damn well stayed that way through life, as a Grand Duke remained a Grand Duke from conception until resurrection. You could move horizontally within your social class without opposition, but vertically out of it, in the Mediterranean swim as in Mayfair, only with great luck and more sweat. Gauche American maidens did sometimes manage to marry into titled European families, but their own families had to be pretty solidly established to bring it off, or at least stinking rich, and wealth, although never frowned upon in the proper hands, was considered vulgar in the wrong ones. Girls like Otéro and de Mérode simply did not exist in the public eye except as actresses, a plural form of h–t––r–, even when presenting themselves to it on the arm of Kaiser Wilhelm. In private you could behave or misbehave pretty much as you liked; what came off in your own bedroom or somebody else's bedroom was nobody's business but your own and the other party's. Out in the open, however, the rules were rigid; nice girls did not wear lipstick, smoke cigareets or divide at the crotch, and deviationists from the aristocratic norm like Princess Brouhaha were ostracized by all right-thinking people. That was the way Victoria had ordered it, that was the way it continued to be right up until the outbreak of hostilities following on the assassination of a blueblood at Sarajevo.

World War I not only killed Victorianism, the Czar and nobility as a dominant social group but made the world safe for a kind of democracy that did not come into existence on the Riviera until after the shooting stopped. Until the war, playboys among the plebs were notable mainly for their rarity. . .

After the war, expressions of extroverted idiosyncrasy among wealthy yacht-owners became commonplace without regard to the colour of their corpuscles. Laura Corrigan, a Cleveland hotel switchboard-operator who married a transient guest after a blind date and moved in on something like eighty million dollars when her husband dropped dead a few months later, used to give her dinner guests diamond-studded cigarette cases and diamond bracelets as party favours, plus $500 in pocket money for each port she took them into while patrolling the Mediterranean, and J. Pierpont Morgan had three yachts in keeping with the growth of his fortune: big, bigger and biggest, the last longer than a football field. . .

The South of France even used to be a cheap place to live, for a time between the two World Wars. Rents were fixed at the levels of 1914, the franc hadn't been blown up like a balloon, you could get fried on 'pastis' for next to nothing, the land produced all it needed to feed itself and visitors, and a friend of mine, a painter who found the Left Bank too cold for his fingers in wintertime, could buy a country home near Saint-Tropez for the equivalent of $180. Led by the survivors of Europe's shattered ruling houses who knew about the place from better days, out-of-step emancipates and peculiar numbers of all kinds gravitated to Provence and the Provençal coastline for more than forty years: poets, painters, Existentialists, opium eaters, Algerian rug peddlers, remittance men, soothsayers, strip-teasers, avant-garde actors, homosexuals, bums, beats, writers, gypsies, trick bicycle riders, unemployed mahouts and Isadora Duncan, who was romantically strangled to death on the Promenade des Anglais in Nice when a flowing scarf she wore around her neck became entangled in a wheel of the car in which she was a passenger. To borrow a line from F. Scott Fitzgerald, you could get away with more on the Riviera, and whatever happened always seemed to have something to do with Art.

. . . fair years to waste, years that I can't honestly regret,
in seeking the eternal Carnival by the Sea.

From: Early Success *by F. Scott Fitzgerald*

HULLABALOOBALAY

Me fa-ther kept a board-in' house Hul-la-ba-loo-ba-
-lay. ___ Hul-la-ba-loo-ba-la-ba-lay; The
board-in' house was on the quay. Hul-la-ba-loo-ba-lay. ___

The boarding house was on the quay;
   Chorus.
The lodgers were nearly all at sea;
   Chorus.

A flash young fellow called Shallow Brown,
   Chorus.
Followed me Mother all round the town,
   Chorus.

Me Father said, 'Young man, me boy,'
   Chorus.
To which he quickly made reply,
   Chorus.

Next day when Dad was in the Crown,
   Chorus.
Mother ran off with Shallow Brown.
   Chorus.

Me Father slowly pined away,
   Chorus.
For Mother came back on the following day.
   Chorus.

GOOD MORNING, LADIES ALL

SOLOIST

Now a long good-bye to you my dear, with a

CHORUS SOLOIST

heave - oh haul And a last fare-well, and a

CHORUS

long fare-well, And good morn-ing, la - dies all.

2. For we're outward bound to New York town;
    Chorus: With a heave –
    And you'll wave to us till the sun goes down.
    Chorus: And good morning –

3. And when we're back again in London Docks
    Chorus: With a heave –
    All the pretty girls will come in Flocks
    Chorus: And good morning –

4. And Poll, and Jane and Sue will say
    Chorus: With a heave –
    'Oh here comes Jack with his three years' pay'
    Chorus: And good morning –

5. So a long good-bye to you, my dear,
    Chorus: With a heave –
    And a last farewell, and a long farewell.
    Chorus: And good morning –

THE GUARDIAN

Peter Heaton

The Mediterranean is almost too well-known as a cruising-ground for yachts. Whether in description of its varied charms (and hazards) or in navigational information, the field – or perhaps I should call it the sea – has been thoroughly covered. However, the following incidents, though set against that cobalt backdrop, are I think, of sufficiently diverting a nature to warrant inclusion here, and will at least either remind the experienced or inform the newcomer to the region, of the mixture of humour and frustration, of the sense of hopelessness coupled with a pleasant (if slow) acceptance – resignation perhaps – that characterises dealings with many of the local inhabitants.

The people to whom I am referring, indeed the country, had better remain anonymous – it matters little; although the experienced will probably guess the latter without difficulty. You can leave a yacht afloat all the year round for a surprisingly small payment; but (at least in the country of which I speak) a 'guardian' is required. This does not mean a resident 'skipper' or paid hand. A part-time guardian is all that is needed.

When I first started cruising in the Mediterranean I had therefore to find a 'guardian'. The first lasted but a month. He explained that he was kept so busy by his regular employer (a wealthy American, who insisted on a spotless hull and gleaming, unblemished varnish *all* the time) that he had regretfully to give up looking after me. His successor, a friend of his, seemed to be the perfect answer. Good-looking, intelligent and very, very polite. However, he too left, or rather I had to dispense with his services. On rejoining the yacht after the winter, I found my dinghy had been stolen. I looked for my 'guardian' only to find he was working on a 'marina' some hundred and fifty miles away and had been there for three months! He was, however, due to return in a week.

I sought the advice of the owner of a local yacht yard. 'Oh they are all bad these fellows – better stick to the bad one you know – no point in changing.' Not convinced, I asked a local acquaintance who had many relations in the neighbourhood. He at once found me a 'retired' sailor, resplendent in white trousers and yachting cap. 'He will be much better,' said my friend, 'he is very serious.' I engaged him. Two days later, having occasion to visit the yacht yard I told the owner what I had done. 'But that is terrible!' he said, 'a bad man who is *serious*!'

However, my new man seemed a great improvement. He was at least about, and he was certainly conscientious. The only trouble was that he was unable to stand up to authority; for when I revisited the harbour at the start of the next season, not only was there no dinghy; there was no yacht!

In due course I found out that the harbour had been 'taken over' by the local yacht club and those boats whose owners were not members, had been arbitrarily shifted to a nearby port. My 'serious' man had, it appeared, made no effort to prevent this; neither had he seen fit to inform me of what was going on.

Two things had to be done. First I joined the Yacht Club (not as easy a manœuvre as one might suspect). Secondly I fired the 'serious' man.

My next 'guardian' was at least a contrast. Tall, athletic and twenty-five years of age, he exuded confidence. He was also very proud of the yacht. I had been using old motor tyres as fenders. 'Those must go,' he announced, 'it looks bad.' They did look bad I agreed, and six (very expensive) sizable new ones arrived. The same with mooring lines. Old weather-stained warps disappeared to be replaced by gleaming nylon. He next turned his attention to the hull, suggesting improvements, each one more extensive – and of course more costly. I soon found that for each job that I commissioned a sum, albeit small, found its way to my guardian. All quite normal and to be expected. On joining the yacht for the following season he informed me that the local yacht yard had gone broke. However, I was fortunate in that a friend of his had acquired the concession and would do any work I wanted; and, by coincidence, this friend was on the quay and I could see him there and then. Having managed not to commit myself too deeply, I walked round to the old yacht yard. It was far from going broke – it was flourishing. However, during the winter, some conversion of the harbour had resulted in it losing its slipway. 'If you are to work on my boat, how can you slip her?' I asked the owner. 'Oh,' he said, 'the new fellow has a large crane and I use that.' 'I see,' I said thoughtfully, 'but if the new fellow wants all your business (including mine) what is to stop him refusing you the use of the crane?' 'He won't do that,' came the reply, 'you see – I am his only customer!'

Oh, well! . . .

CHASING THE WHITE WHALE

From *Moby Dick*, Herman Melville

At daybreak, the three mastheads were punctually manned afresh.

'D'ye see him?' cried Ahab after allowing a little space for the light to spread.

'See nothing, sir.'

'Turn up all hands and make sail! he travels faster than I thought for; – the top-gallant sails! – aye, they should have been kept on her all night. But no matter – 'tis but resting for the rush.'

Here be it said, that this pertinacious pursuit of one particular whale, continued through day into night, and through night into day, is a thing by no means unprecedented in the South Sea fishery. For such is the wonderful skill, prescience of experience, and invincible confidence acquired by some great natural geniuses among the Nantucket commanders, that from the simple observation of a whale when last descried, they will, under certain given circumstances, pretty accurately foretell both the direction in which he will continue to swim for a time, while out of sight, as well as his probable rate of progression during that period. And, in these cases, somewhat as a pilot, when about losing sight of a coast, whose general trending he well knows, and which he desires shortly to return to again, but at some further point; like as this pilot stands by his compass, and takes the precise bearing of the cape at present visible, in order the more certainly to hit aright the remote, unseen headland, eventually to be visited: so does the fisherman, at his compass, with the whale; for after being chased, and diligently marked, through several hours of daylight, then, when night obscures the fish, the creature's future wake through the darkness is almost as established to the sagacious mind of the hunter, as the pilot's coast is to him. . .

The ship tore on; leaving such a furrow in the sea as when a cannon-ball, missent, becomes a ploughshare and turns up the level field.

'By salt and hemp!' cried Stubb, 'but this swift motion of the deck creeps up one's legs and tingles at the heart. This ship and I are two brave fellows! – Ha! ha! Someone take me up, and launch me, spine-wise, on the sea, – for by live-oaks!

'There she blows – she blows! – she blows! – right ahead!'

SEAMEN'S PROVERBS

When the sea hog jumps
Stand to your pumps.

When the glass falls low,
Prepare for a blow;
When it slowly rises high,
Lofty canvas you may fly.

The evening red and morning grey,
Are sure signs of a fine day;
But the evening grey and morning red,
Makes the sailor shake his head.

Seagull, seagull, stay on the strand
We'll ne'er have good weather with thee on the land.

Long foretold, long past,
Short notice, soon past,
Quick rise after low,
Sure sign of stronger blow.

Mackerel sky and Mare's tails,
Make lofty ships carry low sails.

At sea with low and falling glass;
Soundly sleeps the careless ass.
Only when it's high and rising,
Truly rests the prudent wise one.

When rain comes before the wind
Halyards, sheets and braces mind,
But when the wind comes before rain,
Soon you may sail again.

(relating to the hurricane
months in the West Indies) . . . *June, too soon;*
July, stand by;
August, look out you must;
September, remember;
October, all over.

HOW TO MAKE A DREAM COME TRUE

From *The Southseaman*, James Weston Martyr

'George,' said I, 'how much money have you got?'

'About $10, I think,' said George, beginning to feel in his pockets.

'No. I mean – in all the world,' I said.

George is one of those solid loyal souls who, when a friend asks him for information, will do his best to answer with candour and with care, without bothering himself about reasons. My question probed deep into George's most private and vital affairs, but it did not make him flinch. Instead, he thought a little while, and then, said he, 'If I sold my bits of shares and things, and cashed in everything I've got, I could raise, I think, about $5000.'

'Good,' said I. 'You're richer than I thought. The savings of my life, with all I can beg, borrow, and steal, would come to about $4000. Now, George, lend me your ear. As we know, the price of yachts in America is appalling. But there are other countries in the world where a well-built boat can even now be bought fairly cheaply. Suppose we bought one, George, and brought her over here and sold her? I think the profit on the venture would make it fully worth our while.'

George, as I said before, is a solid soul. 'The freight and duty would kill the thing,' said he. 'Yes – dead. Otherwise it's a sound notion.'

'We could save the freight,' said I, 'by sailing her over here ourselves. And I'll find out about the duty.'

'Means chucking our jobs; and you forget the tariff wall they've built around this country. It's high, my boy; and there isn't a loophole in it.'

'I'll inquire about the duty, as I've said. But, as for our jobs – are you in love with yours, George?'

'It stinks in my nostrils.'

'Then, why worry about throwing it up? If this scheme is as good as I am beginning to think it is—— Why, we needn't stop at *one*! We could build a bigger boat out of the profits on the first, and then—— You see, the thing goes on ad infinitum. Lord! What a life! Sailing boats across the Atlantic – and making our fortunes out of it. Think of it, George!'

'Yes,' said George, unmoved. 'I'll think of it; but carefully. And then maybe – we'll see.'

George is six feet three and weighs nearly a ton, so it is hard to excite him. But when we found there actually *was* a hole in the tariff wall, and that vessels, sailing in on their own bottoms, could get through it – duty free – well, then

George began to move. And George in motion was impressive, and he proved himself then to be a man of action, which I decidedly am not.

Mine was the idea, but to George is all the credit due for executing it. He wrote, concerning that vital point of 'duty', to Government officials of whose existence I had never even heard. And, what is more, he obtained from these imposing personages written replies confirming the good news about the hole in the wall. Then he wrote to all the boat-builders in the world. At least I think he did, for there were very many letters; and in time the answers to them began to reach us. All business correspondence leaves me as a rule extremely cold; but these boat-builders' letters were all wonderful, and I read them with delight. For they talked of such things as limber strakes, spirketting, planksheers, hanging-knees, and wales, not to mention reef-pendant cleets and trestletrees; and one man even mentioned a martingale, a word I have always loved. I said so to George. Said he: 'Yes. But I want you to read that letter carefully. It's from a firm in Sheldon, Nova Scotia, and it seems to me they are the very people we've been looking for. Martingales sound fine, I know, but the point about that letter is, it contains an offer to build us a 45 ft schooner for $6000. And $6000 is about half the price of a similar boat in New York to-day! In fact, if you think the construction they propose is satisfactory – well, I'm ready, if you are, to go ahead and tell 'em to build.'

I did not understand, when George said this, that the dream of my life was coming true at last. Things do not, somehow, happen quite like that, and my realisation of the truth was therefore slow. There were many more letters to send to Sheldon and many more replies to receive concerning details of construction, materials, fittings, and design before the climax came. So a month passed by, and found us still with no definite agreement with the builders and the contract for our vessel yet unsigned. And then, one day when we felt ourselves foundering under a mass of ever-growing correspondence, George stood up and spoke his mind.

'It's no good all this writing. We're in for this thing now, so let's do it properly. You'll have to resign and go to Sheldon and settle things on the spot. Tell 'em exactly what we want – and when they make up their minds what they'll do it for, sign the contract and get them going ahead with the work. You'll be there then all the time while she's building, so that nothing should go wrong. And when you're ready I'll take a fortnight's holiday, and we'll sail her down here and sell her.'

Thus did we ingenuously plan. I parted, indeed, from my down-town broker with a very great joy in my heart; and I bought a ticket for Sheldon. But from this precise point onwards a great many things were to happen to us that had not been arranged. For the building of a ship, like the wooing of a girl, is a chancy and uncertain proceeding. And we were to find it so.

For instance: I sat in my railway carriage, waiting to depart, with an eye open for George, who was coming to say good-bye. At the very last moment he appeared, laden with large bags, which he threw at me.

'What's all this, George?' said I. 'Something I've forgotten?'

'No,' said he. 'I couldn't stand any more of it. This is my gear. I'm coming too.'

George, it transpired, had abandoned banking – for ever.

Whither, O splendid ship, thy white
sails crowding,
Leaning across the bosom of
the urgent west.

From: A Passer-by *by Robert Bridges*

A BALLAD OF JOHN SILVER   John Masefield

We were schooner-rigged and rakish, with a long and lissome hull,
And we flew the pretty colours of the cross-bones and the skull;
We'd a big black Jolly Roger flapping grimly at the fore,
And we sailed the Spanish Water in the happy days of yore.

We'd a long brass gun amidships, like a well-conducted ship,
We had each a brace of pistols and a cutlass at the hip;
It's a point which tells against us, and a fact to be deplored,
But we chased the goodly merchant-men and laid their ships aboard.

Then the dead men fouled the scuppers and the wounded filled the chains,
And the paint-work all was spatter-dashed with other people's brains,
She was boarded, she was looted, she was scuttled till she sank.
And the pale survivors left us by the medium of the plank.

O! then it was (while standing by the taffrail on the poop)
We could hear the drowning folk lament the absent chicken-coop;
Then having washed the blood away, we'd little else to do
Than to dance a quiet hornpipe as the old salts taught us to.

O! the fiddle on the fo'c's'le, and the slapping naked soles,
And the genial 'down the middle, Jake, and curtsey when she rolls!'
With the silver seas around us and the pale moon overhead,
And the look-out not a-looking and his pipe-bowl glowing red.

Ah! the pig-tailed, quidding pirates and the pretty pranks we played,
All have since been put a stop-to by the naughty Board of Trade;
The schooners and the merry crews are laid away to rest,
A little south the sunset in the Islands of the Blest.

DO YOU CALL THIS PLEASURE?

From *The Falcon on the Baltic*, E. F. Knight

At eight we found ourselves in the midst of steep and dangerous-looking rollers, so we surmised that we were approaching the banks, and were in shallow water. Our lead proved this to be the case. There are few worse coasts than those of Holland; the shores are so low and destitute of landmarks, and have such perilous sands extending far seawards, that the mariner who approaches them in thick weather often has a very anxious time of it.

We saw that it would be exceedingly difficult for us to make a land-fall and distinguish the lights on such a night, so not daring to run in further towards the outlying shoals, we decided to lie to till morning.

With two-reefed main-sail and fore-sail to windward, the little boat behaved wonderfully well. Great seas with breaking crests thundered down upon her one after another, often seeming as if they must inevitably overwhelm us; but the 'Falcon' rose to them all without fuss, with an easy motion as of a boat conscious of her seaworthiness. After we had watched her behaviour for a while, she imparted her confidence to us. We felt that it would need a much worse sea than any we were likely to encounter this night to endanger her. Besides, I still had sufficient faith in the clerk of the weather to believe that nothing very serious in the way of bad weather was coming. I must not forget to give due praise to the little dinghy, who behaved very well; and though much more fussy than the 'Falcon', she never lost her head.

But there was some danger for us from big steamers on so obscure a night, so we lit our side lights and kept two-hour watches in turns.

No water came over the vessel, but plenty came through her. She leaked terribly, and we were pumping the whole while. Our arms ached for a week after this experience. The night was anything but a pleasant one; it rained, it blew, it was cold, and our position was rather an insecure one.

As I kept my watch in dripping oilies, pumping hard with one hand, holding on with the other, and peering through the obscurity on the look-out for those murderous nuisances the screw steamers, I became meditative.

I called to mind a luxurious friend of mine who had once – only once – slept out with me in an open boat on the Medway one chilly spring night. I was sleeping soundly on the bottom boards, when a melancholy voice calling out my name awakened me. I opened my eyes and beheld standing before me in the boat a spectral form shrouded with the white mist of the river. It was my friend, who, unable to sleep, had risen from his couch among the ballast.

'Well, what is it?' I asked.

'My good friend,' he said sadly, 'do you call this pleasure?'

The wretch had awakened me from my happy slumbers to put me this question!

'And now,' I asked myself, 'is this pleasure?' My conscience replied in the decided negative. 'Then what the dickens am I here for?' and I called to mind many wise saws of the sea, such as: 'A sailor's life is a dog's life,' 'Who'd sell a farm and go to sea?' 'What the dickens am I here for?' I asked myself again, seeing that I might be safe and comfortable at home.

Then, glancing round to see that no steamer was near, I dived below, had a tot of rum, lit a pipe, and returned on deck to my duties. Feeling more comfortable, I now found a satisfactory reply to my question. 'This is not exactly pleasure,' I told myself; 'but such a night is an exception in a long cruise. Bad weather now and then makes the pleasant days all the more enjoyable; besides, yachting would be no more exciting than a voyage on a Thames penny steamer if the weather was always fine. And now for that confounded pump again.'

So passed the uncomfortable night. About an hour before dawn I turned into my bunk and fell asleep.

LINES ON YACHT SALESMANSHIP
AT A BOAT SHOW

Anon

This yacht will turn
upon a sixpence, or a dime,
a groat or centime; anyway
it matters not, the turn is still as small.

She is not dear
for what she is, the sails alone
are worth the price; the engine's free!
You'll not find better value in this hall!

The hull is glass
(most of our boats are G.R.P.)
though some may be of steel; but those
that are of wood are very, very small.

We have a scheme
for easy payment for three years
notice her beam (sta–bil–ity)
The most important feature of them all!

May I arrange a trial for an hour?
(a test both under sail and under power)
But ev'ry-one is wanting one of these
so why not place an order right away?
You will? Good! My assistant, Mister Paul
will take the order. Here please! Mister Paul!

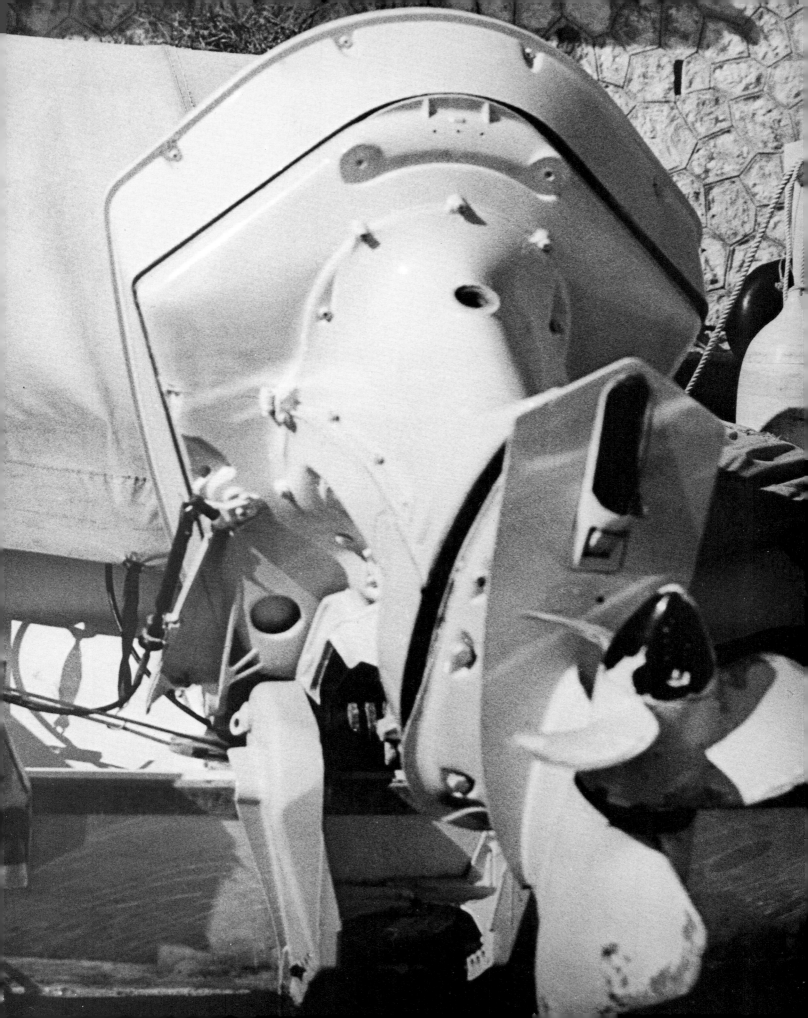

15th August 1660 – Found the King gone this morning by five of the clock to see a Dutch pleasure boat below bridge.

8th November 1660 – Commissioner Pett and I went on board the yacht, which indeed is one of the finest things that ever I saw for neatness and room in so small a vessel. Mr Pett is to make one to outdo this for the honour of his country which I fear he will scarce better.

13th January 1661 – She will be a pretty thing and much beyond the Dutchman.

21st May 1661 – The King was down the river with his yacht this day for pleasure to try it; and as I hear, Commissioner Pett's do prove better than the Dutch one and that that his brother built.

14th September 1661 – Comes a great deal of company to take my wife and I out by barge to show them the King and Duke's yachts. So I was forced to go forth with them, and we had great pleasure seeing all four yachts, viz., these two and the two Dutch ones.

2nd March 1663 – We went down four or five miles with extraordinary pleasure, it being a fine day and a brave gale of wind, and had some oysters brought us aboard newly taken, which were excellent, and ate with great pleasure. There also coming into the river two Dutchmen, we sent a couple of men on board, and bought three Holland's cheeses, cost 4d. apiece excellent cheeses.

4th May 1663 – Meeting the King we followed him into the park where he and Mr Coventry talked of building a new yacht which the King is resolved to have built out of the privy purse he having some contrivance of his own.

3rd September 1663 – To Sir W. Batten who is going this day for pleasure to the Downes. At my lady's desire with them by coach to Greenwich where I went aboard with them on the 'Charlotte' yacht. The wind being fresh I believe they will be sicke enough, besides that she is mighty troublesome on the water.

17th August 1665 – To the 'Bezan' yacht where Sir W. Batten, Sir J. Minnes, My Lord Brouncker and myself with some servants embarked in the yacht and down we went most pleasantly. Short of Gravesend it grew calm, and so we came to an anchor, and to supper mighty merry, and after it, being moonshine we out of the cabbin to laugh and talk, and then as we grew sleepy, went in and upon velvet cushions of the King's that belong to the yacht fell to sleep.

18th August 1665 – Up about 5 o'clock and dressed ourselves, and to sayle again down to the Soveraigne at the buoy at the Nore and thence to Sheernesse. Thence with great pleasure up the Meadeway, our yacht contending with

Commissioner Petts, wherein he met us from Chatham, and he had the best of it.

18th September 1665 – By breake of day we came within sight of the fleete which was a very fine thing to behold, being above 100 ships great and small. Among others the 'Prince', in which My Lord Sandwich was. When we called by her side his Lordshipp was not stirring, so we come to an anchor a little below his ship, thinking to have rowed on board him, but the wind and tide was so strong against us that we could not get up to him – no, though rowed by a boat of the 'Prince's' that came to us to tow us up; at last however he brought us within a little way, and then they flung out a rope to us from the 'Prince', and so come on board; but with great trouble time and patience it being very cold.

Sir W. Penn stayed to dine and did so, but the wind being high the ship did make me sicke, so I could not eat anything almost.

And so to our yacht again. No sooner come into the yacht, though overjoyed at the good work we have done to-day but I was overcome with sea-sickness so that I began to spue soundly, and so continued for a good while, till at last I went into the cabbin, and shutting my eyes my trouble did cease that I fell asleep, which continued till we come into Chatham River where the water was smooth, and then I rose and was very well.

A 'YACHT' RACE

An account of a race between Charles and his brother the Duke of York for a wager of one hundred pounds. This historic event in yachting history is chronicled by John Evelyn:

'1st October 1661 – I sail'd this morning with his Majesty in one of his yachts (or pleasure boats) vessells not known among us til the Dutch East India Company presented that curious piece (Mary) to the King, being very excellent sailing vessells. It was on a wager betweene his other new pleasure boats, built frigate like, and one of the Duke of York's; the wager one hundred pounds; the race from Greenwich to Gravesend and back. The King lost in going, the wind being contrary, but sav'd the stakes in returning. There were divers noble persons and lords on board, his Majesty sometimes steering himselfe. His barge and kitchen boate attended. I brake fast this morning with the King at return in his smaller vessel, he being pleas'd to take me and onely foure more, who were noblemen, with him; but din'd in his yacht, where we all eat together with his Majesty.'

It is curious that there is no mention of this match in Pepys's *Diary*. For some reason Pepys must have intentionally omitted the account, since the race was, without doubt, a subject of general gossip – possibly he was disgruntled at not being one of the Royal party!

151

THE WILD REGIONS OF CAPE HORN

From *Sailing alone around the world*, Captain Joshua Slocum

I saw now only the gleaming crests of the waves. They showed white teeth while the sloop balanced over them. 'Everything for an offing,' I cried, and to this end I carried on all the sail she would bear. She ran all night with a free sheet, but on the morning of March 4th the wind shifted to south-west, then back suddenly to north-west, and blew with terrific force. The 'Spray' stripped of her sails then bore off under bare poles. No ship in the world could have stood up against so violent a gale. Knowing that this storm might continue for many days, and that it would be impossible to work back to the westward along the coast outside of Tierra del Fuego, there seemed nothing to do but to keep on and go east about, after all. Anyhow, for my present safety the only course lay in keeping her before the wind. And so she drove south-east, as though about to round the Horn, while the waves rose and fell and bellowed their never-ending story of the sea; but the Hand that held these held also 'Spray'. She was running now with a reefed forestaysail, the sheets flat amidship. I paid out two long ropes to steady her course and to break combing seas astern, and I lashed the helm amidship. In this trim she ran before it, shipping never a sea. Even while the storm raged at its worst, my ship was wholesome and noble. My mind as to her seaworthiness was put to ease for aye.

When all had been done that I could do for the safety of the vessel, I got to the fore-scuttle, between seas, and prepared a pot of coffee over a wood fire, and made a good Irish stew. Then, as before and afterward on the 'Spray', I insisted on warm meals. In the tide-race off Cape Pillar, however, where the sea was marvellously high, uneven, and crooked, my appetite was slim, and for a time I postponed cooking. (Confidentially, I was seasick!)

The first day of the storm gave the 'Spray' her actual test in the worst sea that Cape Horn or its wild regions could afford, and in no part of the world could a rougher sea be found than at this particular point, namely, off Cape Pillar, the grim sentinel of the Horn.

Farther offshore, while the sea was majestic, there was less apprehension of danger. There the 'Spray' rode, now like a bird on the crest of a wave, and now like a waif deep down in the hollow between seas; and so she drove on. Whole days passed, counted as other days, but with always a thrill – yes of delight.

THE TRAIL THAT IS ALWAYS NEW

From *The Long Trail*, Rudyard Kipling

It's North you may run to the rime-ringed sun
*   Or South to the blind Horn's hate;*
Or East all the way into Mississippi Bay,
*   Or West to the Golden Gate –*
*   Where the blindest bluffs hold good, dear lass,*
*   And the wildest tales are true,*
*   And the men bulk big on the old trail, our own trail, the out trail,*
*   And life runs large on the Long Trail – the trail that is always new.*

O the blazing tropic night, when the wake's a welt of light
*   That holds the hot sky tame,*
And the steady fore-foot snores through the planet-powdered floors
*   Where the scared whale flukes in flame!*
*   Her plates are flaked by the sun, dear lass,*
*   And her ropes are taut with the dew,*
*   For we're booming down on the old trail, our own trail, the out trail,*
*   We're sagging south on the Long Trail – the trail that is always new.*